Vintage Cleveland

By James A. Toman

Photographs of Yesteryear

Publishing Information

Published by:
Cleveland Landmarks Press, Inc.
13610 Shaker Boulevard, Suite 503
Cleveland, Ohio 44120-1592
www.clevelandbook.com
(216) 658 4144

ISBN: 978-0-936760-25-4

LIBRARY OF CONGRESS NUMBER: 2008907277

Designed by:
John Yasenosky, III

Printed by:
Bookmasters
Ashland, Ohio

Table of Contents

Introduction & Acknowledgments

Change is an inescapable reality. Individuals undergo continual change, from infancy through childhood, from adolescence to adulthood, and then on to old age. Similarly in flux is their environment. That is particularly true of cities, where the aggregation of people poses ever changing and often competing needs and aspirations. Cleveland, Ohio, is no exception. Over its more than two centuries, Cleveland has changed from a tiny settlement on the bank of the Cuyahoga River to the principal city in a combined statistical area of 2.896 million people.

Many individuals take comfort from the familiar, and they tend to focus on elements in their environment that are seemingly permanent. What is present today seems always to have been there. Memories of earlier landscape features fade as time passes. While older family members can help the next generation in understanding what was, these recollections and anecdotes are typically sketchy and partial. Images add another layer of comprehension.

The camera has proven to be the indispensable tool for recording how the march of time has changed the face of the city. The Cleveland Public Library and the Western Reserve Historical Society have long been the archives in which Cleveland's rich photographic record has been stored. More recently, Cleveland State University (CSU), through the Special Collections Division of its University Library, has joined their ranks as a primary source of photographic records. Through the Special Collections' Cleveland Memory project (www.clevelandmemory.org) its ever-growing repository has been made readily accessible to the public.

Special Collections has been the recipient of many bequests, and this album of Cleveland photographs is almost totally indebted to the 2003 bequest of Bruce Young. Young was a long-time educator in the Garfield Heights City Schools and an avid buyer of Cleveland negative collections. For many years, he sold copies of some of these historic prints at shows and in the shopping malls throughout Greater Cleveland. He called his enterprise Photographs of Yesteryear, and hence the subtitle of this book.

While his collection, consisting of tens of thousands of images, was derived from many sources (not all of which are clearly documented), probably the most significant of these was the aerial and transportation photography of Robert Runyon, a photographer with the old Cleveland *News*. Bruce Young made sure that the wonderful images he painstakingly collected were preserved, and for that he is owed lasting thanks. All the photos in this book are from CSU's Bruce Young Collection, unless noted otherwise.

Thanks also must go to Bill Barrow, the head of Special Collections at CSU, for his leadership in acquiring, organizing, and making available this treasure trove of Cleveland history. Thanks also goes to Lynn Duchez-Bycko, whose knowledge, efficiency, and friendly support makes working with Special Collections a truly satisfying and enjoyable experience.

My personal thanks also goes to my Cleveland Landmarks Press partner, Greg Deegan, for helping put this book together; to John Yasenosky, III, for designing it; to my other CLP partners Dan and Kathy Cook for supporting it; and to my sister Marjorie Hargus, who has supported me in every venture I have ever undertaken. I cannot imagine a better big sister.

James A. Toman

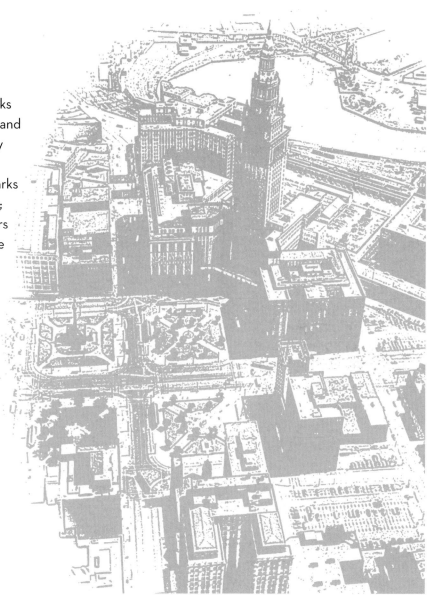

Cleveland Skyline

People gazing at the Cleveland skyline during the 1920s would see a few substantial buildings, but no building really stood out from the others. The tallest building in the city in 1927 was the Ohio Bell Building (now the AT&T Building) on Huron Road. It rose 24 stories and 365 feet.

The next tallest buildings during that era were all rather similar in height. In second place was the 1924, 289-foot, 22-story Union Trust (now Huntington) Building on Euclid Avenue at East Ninth Street. In third place was the 1925 Standard Building at St. Clair Avenue and Ontario Street. It numbered 20 stories and rose 282 feet. Then came the 1922 B. F. Keith Building on Euclid Avenue and East 17th Street (22 stories and 272 feet), and in fifth place was the 1922 Cleveland Discount (now Superior) Building on Superior Avenue just west of East Ninth Street. It was 20 stories and 270 feet in height.

Then the Terminal Tower on Public Square, dedicated in 1930, significantly changed the downtown profile. Rising 52 stories and 708 feet, with an additional 65 feet for its flagpole, the Tower nearly doubled the height of the Ohio Bell Building. Even more noteworthy was that the Terminal Tower was the tallest building in the United States outside New York City, and the eighth tallest overall. For the next 35 years, nothing new joined the skyline to catch the eye.

That began to change with the development of the Erieview urban renewal area centered on East Ninth Street. In 1964 the 100 Erieview building at East 12th Street and St. Clair Avenue pierced the sky with 40 stories, rising 529 feet. Three years later it was joined by a second Erieview tower, the Anthony J. Celebrezze Federal Office Building on East Ninth Street at Lakeside Avenue. The federal building rose

32 stories and 419 feet. While the Terminal Tower was still dominant, these two additions gave the skyline more than a single focus.

During the 1970s and early 1980s other buildings (the Ameritrust Tower in 1971, the Justice Center in 1976, the National City Center in 1980, One Cleveland Center and Eaton Center in 1983) all added to the impressive character of the downtown skyline. These developments were chiefly in the city's financial district and shifted the skyline focus away from Public Square.

In 1985 Public Square regained some of its lost prominence and with it, the first real challenge to the Terminal Tower's dominance of the skyline. The Standard Oil Building (now 200 Public Square), fronting the southeast quadrant of Public Square, rose 658 feet and 45 stories. While the Terminal still had a 50-foot edge on the newcomer, the huge bulk of the Standard Oil Building offered a sharp contrast to the Tower's slender profile.

In 1991 the Society Center (now Key Center) on the northeast quadrant of Public Square captured the title of the city's tallest. Rising 57 stories and 888 feet (63 stories and 948 feet if the cap and the spire are included) the new bank building easily dominated the city skyline.

The cluster of the three tallest building, all located on Public Square, reinforced the Square as the heart of the city and gave the city a compelling new skyline.

In 1945 the Ohio Bell Building on Huron Road dwarfs its neighbors. When it opened in 1927 it was Cleveland's tallest building, but its reign would be short. By that time the steel framework for the Terminal Tower, then under construction, had already exceeded Ohio Bell in height.

In 1950 the Terminal Tower is the clear focal point of the city's skyline.

In 1970 the Terminal Tower has company in defining the skyline. It is flanked on the left by the Anthony J. Celebrezze Federal Office Building, and on the right by the 100 Erieview Tower.

In 1995 Key Center takes pride of place in the city's downtown skyline.
The Terminal Tower is to its left, and 200 Public Square to its right.

Public Square

Public Square is the heart of Cleveland, the crossroads of the city, and the civic ground on which its citizens meet to mark major events. Laid out by Connecticut Land Company surveyors Seth Pease and Amos Spafford in 1796-1797, it represents for most Clevelanders their most central image of "downtown" Cleveland. Divided into four quadrants and intersected by Superior Avenue and Ontario Street, Public Square itself has had many facelifts over the years, but its essential character has remained unchanged.

Much more obvious have been the many changes in the structures on the Square's perimeter, where the city's three tallest buildings (Key Center, the Terminal Tower, and 200 Public Square) are located. Only three structures in or around the Square pre-date the 20th Century: the 1855 First Presbyterian Church (Old Stone), the 1890 Society for Savings Bank Building, and the 1894 Soldiers and Sailors Monument.

In this view from the late 1880s, the Square's early bucolic nature is evident. An electrically powered streetcar passes through the Square on its way to Woodland Avenue.

This aerial view of Public Square was taken in 1950. The Square looked then much as it had since 1930 when the Terminal Tower Complex was completed.

Old Stone Church, built in 1855, is seen here in 1890. To its left is the Wick Block, which housed the Lyceum Theatre. To the right is the Society for Savings Building under construction.

A temporary Centennial Arch bridges Superior Avenue in 1896. Behind it the Society of Savings Building is festooned to help mark the city's centenary. The Soldiers and Sailors Monument is to the right.

By 1906 Public Square had shed all vestiges of its small-town past. This bustling view looks west along Superior Avenue. The shadowy form at the extreme left of the photo is the Rockefeller Building at West Sixth Street.

The Soldiers and Sailors Monument, the work of Cleveland sculptor Levi Scofield, was dedicated in 1894. It pays tribute to the Clevelanders who served in the Union Army during the Civil War. It is seen here in 1918, its original finish by then begrimed by industrial pollutants. The Williamson Building forms the backdrop.

Looking northeast across Public Square, decorated in honor of
a Grand Army of the Republic convention, one can see the 1892
Cuyahoga Building to the right and the 1858 Federal Courthouse
to the left. The old courthouse was demolished in 1905.

Horse-drawn carriages await patrons leaving the Forest City House.
The hotel, at the southwest quadrant of the Square, was one of the
city's finest. It served the traveler from 1852 to 1916.

Until 1930 Public Square's southwest quadrant sported a fountain and pond bisected by a short pedestrian bridge.

In 1915 apart from the Forest City House, the southwest quadrant of the Square was framed by low-rise multi-tenant buildings and a plethora of advertising. That would change in 1919 when brothers Oris Paxton and Mantis James Van Sweringen put their plans for a new union railroad station into high gear.

The Cuyahoga Building and the 1900 Williamson Building frame the southeastern edge of Public Square. Both were imploded in 1982 to make way for the new headquarters building for Standard Oil of Ohio.

It is 1929. Looking east across the northeast quadrant of Public Square, one can just make out the public rostrum at the bottom of the image and to its right one of the four 1901 pagoda waiting stations that Cleveland Railway built on the Square. To the left is the 1899 Chamber of Commerce Building. Beyond is the Mall, which was not finally cleared until 1935. The Music Hall addition to Public Auditorium is nearing completion.

Public Square was ideally suited to its role as a transit hub, each quadrant serving as the turn-around for several of the city's streetcar and bus lines.
This is a scene from 1945. The Moses Cleaveland statue stands at the center of the southwest quadrant.

If the snow does not make clear the time of year, then the Christmas trees on the lamp poles should. Clevelanders are a hardy bunch, and so the wintry conditions in this 1947 scene do not deter them from their appointed rounds.

Public Square is aglow in lights in this Christmas 1957 scene. The large lighted tree is on the Higbee Building, and the stars and vertical lights adorn Hotel Cleveland.

The completion of the Terminal Tower in 1930 saw downtown development come to a halt. The Great Depression had arrived, and the economy was in tatters. It was not until 1956 that the city would see its next skyscraper rise. Here in 1957 work is underway installing the glass curtain wall on the 21-story Illuminating Building (now 55 Public Square). The older Illuminating Building (now 75 Public Square) is to the right.

The 1913 Marshall Building (later known as 1 Public Square) and the 1895 Mohawk Building (later known as 100 Public Square) lined the edge of the Square's northwest quadrant. They were razed in 1989 to make way for a new headquarters building of Ameritrust. Before construction could begin, however, Ameritrust merged into KeyBank, and the site of these two veteran structures became a surface parking lot. *(Cleveland Press Collection)*

In 1946 the Terminal Tower asserts its dominance in the Public Square neighborhood as it casts its shadow across Public Square, partially obscuring the Williamson Building.

Terminal Tower Complex

The most dramatic change in Public Square was the construction of the Terminal Tower Group. The complex began in the minds of Oris Paxton and Mantis James van Sweringen as a modest interurban station at the southwest quadrant of Public Square. And then, in typical van Sweringen fashion, the idea blossomed into a skyline-changing and nationally recognized complex that is now listed on the National Register of Historic Places.

Actual construction on the site began in 1916 with the Hotel Cleveland (now Renaissance Cleveland) building at the corner of the Square and Superior Avenue. It continued with the Terminal Tower building; the Higbee department store; the Medical Arts (now Republic), Builders Exchange (now Guildhall), and Midland buildings on Prospect Avenue; the Cleveland Union Terminal railroad passenger station; and ended with the 1934 dedication of the main United States Post Office Building between Prospect Avenue and Huron Road.

Interconnected by a series of below-street level passageways, the development transformed Public Square, boosted civic pride, and provided the city with a landmark that quickly gained national recognition.

The complex cost $179 million. If it were built today, its price tag would be $2.14 billion.

In this 1917 view Hotel Cleveland has been completed. All the other buildings in this scene, west of Ontario Street, bisecting the Square at the left, and behind the hotel up to the river's edge, will be razed to make way for the next phases in the Cleveland Union Terminal development.

West Superior Avenue was lined with office buildings and shops. These would all be razed as part of the new union station construction.

Though the buildings on West Superior have been cleared, the bridges that will carry Prospect Avenue and Huron Road are not yet built, and only the support columns for the Cleveland Union Terminal viaduct have been completed.

Construction on the Terminal Tower is well underway in this 1927 view. The area to the right is where the Cleveland Union Terminal facilities will be built.

This view from the south shows the extent of the Cleveland Union Terminal coach yards. Running across the picture is Huron Road. The small building at the center of the scene supports the skylight over the train station's main concourse. The union station was entirely below street level.

The Cleveland Terminal project involved far more than just the downtown property. It also built an electrified rail line stretching from Collinwood on the east to Linndale on the west. At these points steam-powered passenger trains would switch to electric locomotives for the trip into the downtown station. The electrics spared the downtown station the smoke and noise that were inevitable with steam engines. Here an electric engine heads west on the CUT viaduct.

In this aerial view Superior Avenue is to the left, and Prospect Avenue angles to the right. Hotel Cleveland (now the Renaissance Cleveland) is in the foreground.

The Terminal group was designed so that it enfolded the southwest quadrant of Public Square. This is probably the most familiar Terminal scene, the portico serving as a kind of "front porch" for Public Square. Countless civic events, from parades and protests to concerts and commemorations, have been staged there.

This view of the complex has Huron Road running off to the left and Ontario Street angling to the right. The Prospect Buildings (now called the Landmark Office Towers) are in the foreground. The indentations in their facades allowed natural light into the buildings and provided for ventilation in an age before central air conditioning. Today the Landmarks Office Towers are owned by the Sherwin-Williams Company, which operates its world headquarters from there.

Railroad Scenes

Before Cleveland Union Terminal was built, the city's main railroad station was the Union Depot, located at the foot of West Ninth Street. Built in 1866, it chiefly served the New York Central and Pennsylvania railroads whose main tracks ran along the lakefront. At the time of its construction it was said to be the country's largest building under a single roof.

The years took their toll. Constantly exposed to the smoke from the steam engines that idled on the station's tracks, the building exterior was thick with grime, and its facilities had become shabby. These conditions were what led to a 1919 citywide vote endorsing construction of Cleveland Union Terminal. Even after the new station was built, the Pennsylvania Railroad continued to use the old Union Deport until 1953, when it shifted its passenger services to its other facility at East 55th Street and Euclid Avenue. The Pennsylvania never used the new CUT. What remained of the old Union Depot was razed in 1959.

Besides the Pennsylvania, several other railroads serving the city maintained their own stations before CUT came on line. The Baltimore & Ohio and Erie railroads had stations in the Flats, and the Nickel Plate and the Wheeling & Lake Erie railroads along Broadway Avenue.

The 1945 aerial view shows Union Depot at the foot of West Ninth Street. Front Avenue is to its south, and the Memorial Shoreway can be seen crossing over the lakefront tracks to the east.

This is the Union Depot in its original configuration. The view is from the east.

The passenger entrance to Union Depot was on its southern front.
Above the windows is a carved stone bearing the year 1865.
The station opened for business one year later.

In 1952 a Pennsylvania Railroad diesel heads east with three passenger cars in tow. The depot, much of its train shed already gone, is in its last year of operation.

With steam engines belching smoke like this, it is little wonder that Union Depot's once light sandstone walls had been blackened by years of exposure to locomotives idling in and around the station.

Before it moved into CUT, the Baltimore & Ohio Railroad operated its Cleveland passenger service out of this station on Canal Road in the Flats. The station building remains to the present, and some groups hope to restore it as a historical museum.

Before Cleveland Union Terminal, the Erie Railroad had its train shed and passenger station located below the Detroit-Superior Bridge. The roadway to the right leads up to Superior Avenue. The building beyond the bridge is the Western Reserve Building.

The Nickel Plate Railroad became the van Sweringen brothers' first foray into railroad ownership. Naturally their line would use the new CUT station. The old station on Broadway Avenue was torn down.

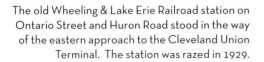

The old Wheeling & Lake Erie Railroad station on Ontario Street and Huron Road stood in the way of the eastern approach to the Cleveland Union Terminal. The station was razed in 1929.

Cleveland's Lakefront

General Moses Cleaveland and his troop of Connecticut Land Company partners arrived at the mouth of the Cuyahoga River in July 1796. The company had bought the Western Reserve lands east of the Cuyahoga River from the State of Connecticut and came west to survey their acquisition. Their purpose was less about establishing a city and more about capitalizing on their investment by finding a commercial hub. The location of the Erie lakefront and the mouth of the Cuyahoga struck them as a propitious site. Several decades before the advent of the railroad, water routes were the key to shipping. And so Cleveland was born.

The idea of utilizing the lake and river for commerce was foremost in the minds of the early settlers, and that concept became the key to development. Waterfront land was not perceived as a site for recreation or residences. It was meant for docks to handle the ships that would bring raw materials to the city and carry its finished products to the east. The lakefront and the riverbanks became lined with loading docks. As the importance of rail transportation grew, the lakefront was crisscrossed with tracks to serve the docks.

The lake also became a site for dredgings and rubbish disposal as the city's edge moved farther into the lake. Cleveland Municipal Stadium and Burke Lakefront Airport are two prominent examples of how landfills were ultimately utilized.

While the idea of using the waterfront property for recreation was not new — Edgewater and Gordon parks testify to this — the idea of using the downtown for similar purposes did not seriously arise until the 1970s. In 1978 the Cleveland Lakefront State Park was established, and the State of Ohio took over management of Edgewater, Gordon, and Euclid Beach parks. Freed from this burden, in 1985 the City of Cleveland unveiled its Inner Harbor plan. It would create a lake basin just east of East Ninth Street and provide walkways and green space where asphalt and parking lots had dominated.

In the years since, the Inner Harbor site became home to the Rock and Roll Hall of Fame and Museum, the Great Lakes Science Center, the William G. Mather Steamship Museum, and Voinovich Park.

In 2004 the Cleveland City Planning Commission endorsed a 50-year project to guide the ongoing transformation of the lakefront, its theme: connecting people to the waterfront. In 2007 the Cleveland Cuyahoga County Port Authority began studying plans which envision moving existing downtown port facilities east to a new landfill area near East 55th Street. Under construction in 2008, the $500 million Flats East Bank development is creating a vibrant mixed-use community at the river's edge. Cleveland's central waterfront is on its way to becoming ever more people-friendly.

The harbor is filled with lake freighters, and hundreds of rail cars are lined up on Whiskey Island, the lakefront area just west of downtown. The scene clearly documents the priority given to commerce and industry on lakefront land. The area in the forefront of the scene is a sewage treatment facility.

Cleveland-Cliffs, Inc., headquartered in Cleveland, operated the largest fleet of ore carriers on the Great Lakes.
Here its ship *Grand Island* is docked at the Hulett unloading complex on Whiskey Island. As lake freighters became self-unloading,
the huge Huletts became artifacts of an earlier industrial age. Two of the four giant machines have been disassembled and saved,
and efforts continue to find a new site where they can be appreciated as part of the city's shipping heritage.

In 1952 the docks west of Cleveland Municipal Stadium are serving a steady stream of lake ore carriers.

The Cleveland and Buffalo (later the Lederer) Terminal and the East Ninth Street pier occupy downtown's central lakefront property. The open area of filled land to the right is the site where Cleveland Municipal Stadium will rise in 1931. These piers were built in 1913 to accommodate lake cruise ships.

The Cleveland and Buffalo (C & B) company operated cruise ships that connected Cleveland with Cedar Point and Toledo to the west and with Buffalo to the east. During the summer months the Cleveland Railway Company ran streetcar service to the foot of East Ninth Street to serve cruise ship passengers.

The East Ninth Street Pier was one of the few downtown places where Clevelanders could easily walk to the lake's edge.
Captain Frank's seafood restaurant at the center of the pier was a long-time favorite spot for dining.

This view illustrates the lakefront area immediately west of the Cuyahoga River and documents the extent to which the railroads dominated the scene. The warren of railroad tracks prohibited any recreational use of the land.

During 1936-1937 the Great Lakes Exposition was held on the Mall, extending down to the lakefront. The expo was intended to showcase Greater Cleveland's products and services, but it also provided visitors a welcome diversion from the worries and dreariness of the Depression years.

During the Great Lakes Exposition, some seven million visitors visited the Expo and the schooners and larger steamships at the lakefront. The attractions made clear the importance of Lake Erie to the local economy.

One people-oriented use of the lakefront was the 1931 construction there of Cleveland Municipal Stadium. As this view indicates, the Stadium was built right at the water's edge.

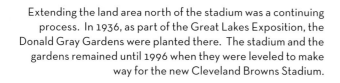

Extending the land area north of the stadium was a continuing process. In 1936, as part of the Great Lakes Exposition, the Donald Gray Gardens were planted there. The stadium and the gardens remained until 1996 when they were leveled to make way for the new Cleveland Browns Stadium.

The Stadium was a good hike from the Public Square transit hub, but on a sunny fall afternoon, that was not a problem. The same walk would be much less pleasant on a windy and snowy December Sunday. Browns' fans, howcver, were not deterred.

The SS *Aquarama* steams into Cleveland harbor.
A former troop ship, the *Aquarama* was rebuilt as a Great
Lakes cruise ship. Between 1957 and 1962, it offered
cruises between Cleveland and Detroit. Later it became a
stationary display in Muskegon, Michigan. It was scrapped
in 2007. *(Cleveland Press Collection)*

The Cuyahoga River made it possible for large lake freighters to deliver their loads of iron
ore directly to the steel plants upriver. Direct shipments like this helped Cleveland to
become a major steel town. The downside of such development, however, was a polluted
river as this scene shows. West 25th Street is in the foreground.

The Cuyahoga River divided the city and made it necessary for Cleveland to become a city of bridges.
In this view from the lakefront are: the Memorial Shoreway Bridge, the Detroit-Superior Bridge,
the Cleveland Union Terminal Viaduct, and the Lorain-Carnegie (now Hope Memorial) Bridge.

Detroit-Superior Bridge

By 1900, getting across the Cuyahoga River, which separated Cleveland's east and west sides, was becoming increasingly more time consuming. The main bridge over the river, the 1878 Superior Viaduct, was a low-level crossing. This meant that it had to have a moveable center span to allow ship traffic on the river to pass through. When the center span swung open, traffic on the bridge surface came to a halt, and long back-ups resulted. The solution was to build a high-level bridge.

County voters approved bonds for a new Detroit-Superior High Level Bridge in 1910, and engineering studies got underway. The new high-level bridge was designed with two decks. The top deck would be for cars and trucks; the bottom one would be for streetcars. Separating the two modes of traffic would speed both on their trip across the river.

Construction was completed in November 1917, and the first streetcars rumbled along the lower deck on December 24. Just over 36 years later, on January 24, 1954, Cleveland's last streetcar crossed the bridge, and soon thereafter the subway portals were sealed over, adding lanes for access to the upper deck.

In recent years the Cuyahoga County Engineer's office has provided free tours of the lower deck on holiday weekends. Thousands of Clevelanders have taken advantage of the opportunity to enjoy a glimpse of the way things were.

Two streetcars, two horse-drawn wagons, and a small truck are at the western end of the old Superior Viaduct. If traffic had always been this light, there probably would not have been any need for a high-level replacement.

This aerial view of the Detroit-Superior Bridge (renamed the Veterans Memorial Bridge in 1989) shows how much higher it stands compared to the old Superior Viaduct, whose stone arches can be seen at the right.

The center span of the Detroit-Superior Bridge was 96 feet above the Cuyahoga River, making it possible for even the largest lake freighters to pass beneath. The lower deck, unused since 1954, carried streetcar traffic to and from the west side of the city.

In 1948 three streetcars travel east on West Superior Avenue, heading for Public Square.
Another is on its way into the subway.

The West Sixth subway portal carried four tracks for streetcars. The two at the left served the lines that would enter and exit the subway on Detroit Avenue at West 29th Street. The two on the right brought streetcars to and from another portal on West 25th Street at Franklin Avenue.

A streetcar is emerging from the Detroit Avenue portal at West 29th Street. These tracks served cars on the Clifton, Detroit, and Fulton lines.

This passenger station at West 25th Street served inbound traffic on the Broadview, State, Pearl, Clark, Lorain, and Madison streetcar lines. The stairs at the left led to the surface of the bridge.

The subway had passenger stations at West Ninth and West 25th streets.
Here passengers await an inbound car at the West Ninth Station.

Car 4127, in service on the Lorain Avenue line, stops at
the West 25th Street subway station.

Euclid Avenue

Euclid Avenue has always been Cleveland's main street, but over the years its role has changed significantly. In the 19th Century it was the boulevard of stately homes, familiarly referred to as "Millionaires' Row." Pressures from the city's commercial interests then encroached on the preserve of the wealthy, and lower Euclid Avenue was transformed into a shopping and entertainment mecca. By the 1960s downtown shopping began to fade due to competition from suburban malls, and one after the other, the city's six department stores closed as did most of their surrounding specialty shops. Euclid Avenue lost much of its glitter.

Euclid Avenue is now entering yet another phase of transformation. The Euclid Avenue Corridor Project began construction in 2005. It has resulted with the thoroughfare being totally rebuilt from Public Square through University Circle, lined with trees and shrubs, its center lanes reserved as a bus rapid transit zone marked by attractive landscaped passenger stations. The HealthLine, as the bus rapid transit line has been named, will connect Public Square with Playhouse Square, Cleveland State University, Cleveland Clinic, and University Circle.

As the avenue reconstruction got underway, and probably spurred by the development, there came a flurry of announcements about renovating some of the vacant buildings along downtown Euclid Avenue into apartments and condominiums. After a century, once again Euclid Avenue will regain some of its earlier residential character, interspersed with offices, restaurants, theatres, and retail.

Euclid Avenue, perhaps more than any other location in the city, testifies to the ever changing nature of the urban cityscape.

THE "ROW"

The 1878 Rufus Winslow house was located at 2409 Euclid Avenue. It was razed in 1926 to make way for the National Town and Country Club building, which later became the main campus building for Fenn College. Known as Fenn Tower and renovated in 2007, today it serves as a Cleveland State University residence hall.

The Sylvester Everett house, just east of East 40th Street was completed in 1887. The 35-room mansion was one of the grandest on the avenue. It was torn down in 1938.

The 1912 Anthony Carlin house at 3233 Euclid Avenue was the last of the great homes to be built in "Millionaires' Row," and it was occupied by the family until 1950. Later it became the headquarters of the International Ladies Garment Workers Union before succumbing to the wreckers' ball to make way for the new headquarters of ATO.

In 1950 some remnants of the "Millionaires' Row" era remained. These homes, just east of Fenn Tower, were from west to east the former residences of Henry Devereux, Samual Mather, Leonard Hanna, Charles Hickox, and William Chisholm. The Devereux house was razed in 1952. The Hanna, Hickox, and Chisholm houses fell in 1958 to make way for the Innerbelt Freeway. The Mather Mansion has survived; it now provides office and meeting space for Cleveland State University.

THE SHOPPING DISTRICT – PUBLIC SQUARE TO EAST 18TH STREET

The 1886 Lennox Building stood at the northeast corner of Euclid Avenue and East Ninth Street. The five-story building featured retail on its ground floor and apartments above. Here it is seen in 1920 bearing a sign announcing that it will soon give way to a mammoth new headquarters for the Union Trust (later Union Commerce and now Huntington) Bank.

The Hickox Building guarded the northwest corner of Euclid Avenue and East Ninth Street. The clock on its tower formerly graced the First Baptist Church that had previously occupied the site. The tall building to the left is the New England Building (now the Garfield Building). The Hickox Building was razed in 1946 to make way for a new Bond's Clothing store.

Two of the tallest buildings ever to be razed in Cleveland were the former homes of the State Bank and Trust and Union Trust just west of East Fourth Street. The properties were sold to the F. W. Woolworth Company in 1945, and the buildings came down to make way for the new Woolworth store.

Cleveland Trust Bank was headquartered on the southeast corner of Euclid Avenue and East Ninth Street. Its 1909 rotunda building still stands and is projected to be a key part of the redevelopment of the entire stretch of East Ninth Street between Euclid and Prospect avenues.

The Arcade is one of Cleveland's most famous buildings. Built in 1890 and connecting Euclid Avenue with Superior Avenue, it had office towers on each end, with a five-story atrium in between. Small shops filled the lower two levels, with offices above. Following a total renovation, in 2001 the Arcade was reconfigured into a Hyatt Regency Hotel, with guest rooms occupying the Superior tower and the upper floor of the central atrium.

In 1946 lower Euclid Avenue is jammed with pedestrians and transit vehicles. This part of the avenue had several stores that sold merchandise at reasonable prices. S.S. Kresge and W.T. Grant stores can be seen at the right of the photo, and a construction fence just beyond marks where a new F.W. Woolworth store is being developed. KB and Rosenblum stores are on the left. One can just make out the famous windmill sign of Mill's Restaurant peeking out from behind the light pole.

The people and vehicles are largely gone from the same scene on a winter's evening, but a few window shoppers check out the holiday window displays in the May Company store on the right.

The brightly decorated May Company store, with reindeer pulling Santa's sleigh and a banner proclaiming "the magic of Christmas at May's" recalls some of the "magic" that permeated all the downtown stores during the busy holiday shopping season.

May Company's Euclid Avenue building is what usually comes to mind when thinking about the department store. May's, however, began its business in Cleveland on Ontario Street, as seen here. When the store opened its new building on Euclid Avenue in 1915, it was connected at the basement level to the original store. To the right of May's is The Bailey Company, and to its left is an F. W. Woolworth store.

Streetcars are tied up from Public Square to past East Sixth Street. The relatively few people waiting in the passenger island suggest that most travelers had probably moved over to Superior or Prospect avenues to catch their ride home. The Kangesser Brothers, Rosenblum, and W.B. Davis clothing stores line the space between the Williamson Building and the Arcade.

On the south side of Euclid Avenue, just west of East Ninth Street stood the Hippodrome Theatre. The 1907 theatre boasted the second largest stage in the country. The theatre also had an entrance from Prospect Avenue. To its east is the main downtown store of the Cleveland clothier Richman Brothers, and to the west the Wm. Taylor and Sons department store. The Hipp and Richman buildings were razed in 1982.

In 1925 a crowd crosses East Ninth Street at Euclid Avenue. They have been guided by the manned traffic tower in the center of the intersection. The tower provided downtown's first traffic signals. It was in place until 1931.

The sidewalks are crowded in this 1938 photo of Playhouse Square, Euclid Avenue and East 14th Street.
Some of the crowd undoubtedly will take in a movie at one of the five theatres in Playhouse Square.

In 1951 Bonwit Teller of New York opened its Playhouse Square store in the former Lindner Coy building. Lindner Coy had consolidated with Sterling and Welch and W. B. Davis two years earlier. Next to Bonwit Teller is the Stouffer Building, then headquarters of Cleveland's famous restaurant chain.

The Hanna Building, on the right, marks the beginning of the theatre district. On the left can be seen signs for the Allen and State theatres. It is 1921, and the theatres of Playhouse Square are in business. The Euclid and Hermitage hotels are at the extreme right (later the site for the Black Angus and then Rusty Scupper restaurants and now for the U.S. Bank building).

The State and Ohio theatres are still doing well in this 1956 scene. Just 13 years later they would be shuttered, and in 1972 they were threatened with demolition. Fortunately the community came together and the theatres were saved. Fully restored in the early 1980s, along with the Allen and Palace theatres, they now form the nucleus of a vibrant and successful Playhouse Square theatre district.

The Stillman Theatre was located just west of East 12th Street, its entrance in the western portion of the Hotel Statler building. This scene dates from 1956. The Stillman would become the first of the major downtown movie theatres to close. That came in 1963.

The B. F. Keith Building and its Palace Theatre opened in 1922, the last of the Playhouse Square theatres to be built. It stands on Euclid Avenue at East 17th Street.

In 1942, the street lights are ablaze but the theatre marquees in
Playhouse Square are dark, accommodating wartime restrictions.

EUCLID AVENUE – MIDTOWN

A Euclid Avenue streetcar is heading east on its trip to Windermere Station. The location is about where today the Innerbelt Freeway passes beneath Euclid Avenue. Fenn Tower is in the background.

Cleveland Arena, on Euclid Avenue just east of East 36th Street, was for many years the home of the Cleveland Barons and then the Crusaders hockey teams. It also briefly hosted the Cleveland Pipers and Cavaliers. Boxing and wrestling matches were held there, and even Alan Freed's Moondog Coronation Ball. After the Coliseum in Richfield was built, the Arena no longer was needed, and it was razed in 1977. *(Cleveland Press Collection)*

The streetcar is passing apartment buildings and the Stonebridge Hotel on the south side of Euclid Avenue west of East 40th Street. The tower of First Methodist Church can be seen in the distance.

Streetcars on the East 55th line are crossing Euclid Avenue. So too are the tracks of the Pennsylvania Railroad which finally elevated them above the intersection in 1915. The building at the right is the East 55th Pennsylvania Station. It was torn down in 1973.

The Cleveland Clinic's first permanent building, on Euclid Avenue at East 93rd Street, dates to 1921, and was the scene of a tragic 1929 fire. The small building gives little evidence of the Clinic's future great growth. In 2008 Cleveland Clinic was named as one of the five best medical centers in the United States.

Traffic is proceeding at a crawl in this November 24, 1950, view of Euclid Avenue at East 77th Street. It was the onset of one of the city's most crippling blizzards. On the left is the Cleveland Playhouse and on the right can be seen the sign for Moe's Main Street, a popular entertainment venue.

This aerial view of the Cleveland Clinic looks south towards Carnegie Avenue. Just about the entire area between Euclid and Carnegie and over to Cedar today is filled with Clinic facilities. So is much of the land north of Euclid to Chester Avenue.

Doan's Corners & University Circle

For the first two thirds of the 20th Century Doan's Corners was considered Cleveland's "second downtown." It was also the western gateway to University Circle. The name originated with Nathaniel Doan who set up shop at the corner of East 107th Street and Euclid Avenue. Over time the area boomed, and it included the block between East 105th and East 107th Streets. The shopping and theatre district actually stretched westward to East 101st Street where downtown's Bailey Company opened the city's first branch department store. The area eventually succumbed to urban decay, and by 1970 most of the district had been leveled and rebuilt for institutional purposes.

It has frequently been observed that Cleveland is a "dual-hub" city. In fact, that name was used to describe the 1980s plans to build a rail rapid transit line connecting Public Square with University Circle — the two hubs. Both are key employment centers, but whereas Public Square is at the heart of the city's commercial, financial, and legal infrastructure, University Circle is the center of its artistic, academic, and cultural life.

The 1880 decision of Western Reserve University (since 1967 Case Western Reserve University) trustees to relocate the college from Hudson, Ohio, to its present location along Euclid Avenue just east of Martin Luther King, Jr., Boulevard was the key event in the formation of what today is Cleveland's cultural center.

Besides the university and its affiliated University Hospitals, the Circle is home to the Cleveland Museum of Art, the Cleveland Orchestra, the Western Reserve Historical Society,

Cleveland Botanical Garden, the Museum of Natural History, the Cleveland Institute of Art, and the Cleveland Institute of Music, among others.

As the first decade of the 21st Century comes to a close, exciting development plans are on the table, and the Circle is poised for an even more robust future.

Shoppers stroll along the sidewalks at Euclid Avenue and East 101st Street in this 1939 scene.

In this night scene, the marquees of the University and Keith theatres can be seen at the left.
They were between East 107th and East 105th streets. In the distance it is just possible to make
out the signs for the Circle and Park theatres, located to the west of East 105th.

A streetcar pulling a trailer car stops at East 105th Street. At the left is the Regent Hotel. The scene looks toward the east. In the distant left is the Fenway Hall Hotel.

This scene looks west from East 105th Street. Hotel Haddam is on the left, and farther west is the Circle Theatre.

Looking east from East 105th Street in 1935, one can see
beyond Doan's Corners to University Circle.

The Elysium is being razed in 1953. It had closed as a skating rink in 1941, and then served as a used car dealership. When it was built, it was the largest skating rink in the country. For a period of time before the Cleveland Arena was built, it was the home of the Barons hockey team.

The Tudor Arms Hotel is under construction. The view looks north along East 107th Street. On the right is John Hay High School, and across the street from it is the old Cathedral Latin High School, now the site for the W. O. Walker Rehabilitation Center.

This aerial view sweeps over the campuses of the Case Institute of Technology and
Western Reserve University; the large cluster of buildings is University Hospitals.

East Ninth & Erieview

From the shore of Lake Erie south to Broadway Avenue, East Ninth Street (originally called Erie Street) was relatively short, yet is was the city's most important downtown north-south street. Today it is the main thoroughfare of the city's financial district.

In 1960 the City of Cleveland announced the Erieview Urban Renewal Plan which would rebuild the area north of Euclid Avenue between East Sixth and East 14th streets. East Ninth Street was the center of this renewal zone, and the street that would witness the most change over the next 25 years.

The Erie Street Cemetery, Cleveland's first public cemetery, dates from 1826. It runs between East Ninth (originally Erie Street and hence the cemetery's name) and East 14th streets, which is at the right edge of the photo. The street on the cemetery's northern boundary is Erie Court; on its southern flank is Sumner Avenue. The Hanna Building is to the right.

Streetcars meet at the intersection of East Ninth Street and Prospect Avenue. The Erie Building on the right was home to the Strand Theatre, one of the city's earliest movie houses. Hotel Winton (later the Carter Hotel) is farther east on Prospect.

The triangular structure in the center of this 1922 photo is the Osborn Building. It is located between Prospect Avenue and Huron Road, just east of East Ninth Street. Today the Osborn is one of the several downtown office buildings that have been converted to residential use.

The six-way intersection at East Ninth Street, Prospect Avenue, and Huron Road was a traffic nightmare. This view looks east. Cars and trackless trolleys are inching their way across East Ninth Street in this 1950 scene. Eventually this problem was addressed by having Huron Road turn onto Prospect just before East Ninth Street.

A procession is entering St. John the Evangelist Roman Catholic Cathedral as Knights of Columbus stand at attention. The cathedral church has occupied the northeast corner of East Ninth Street and Superior Avenue since 1848. The cathedral was rededicated in 1948 following a major enlargement and renovation of the original building.

The Ellington Apartments were situated on the southwest corner of East Ninth Street and Superior Avenue. Across from the Ellington is the city's former Greyhound bus station. The Greyhound property was razed in 1958 to make way for the East Ohio Building, and the Ellington came down in 1967 for the new headquarters of Central National Bank (now a part of Keybank).

This 1945 aerial view looks south over Cleveland's famous mall. In the foreground is Cleveland City Hall. East of the Mall is Public Auditorium, and east of that is the Central Armory. Farther left is East Ninth Street, lined with small nondescript buildings. Everything east of Public Auditorium will come down to make way for the Erieview improvements.

This 1939 view looks south on East Ninth Street from Superior Avenue. The Ellington apartments are on the right. All the buildings seen in this view up to Euclid Avenue in the distance would be razed as part of the Erieview-inspired modernization of the street.

The scene looks down at Lakeside Avenue between East Sixth and East Ninth streets. The dark building in the center is the 1893 Central Armory, the site of many civic events and athletic competitions. The armory was demolished in 1965 to make way for the new federal building.

In 1952 a fire struck the Gillsy Hotel on the east side of East Ninth Street between Superior and Chester avenues. The fire was quickly put out, and the rundown hotel was given a reprieve. Eventually it and Jean's Funny House to its north would be razed for the Investment (now Ohio Savings) Plaza development.

In 1959 the Cleveland Press moved from its old building at East Ninth Street and Rockwell Avenue to this modern facility at the corner of East Ninth Street and Lakeside Avenue. After the Press ceased publication in June 1982, the corner became the site for the North Point 1 building.

In this aerial view of East Ninth Street, the 1900 Rose Building occupies the northwest corner of East Ninth at Prospect Avenue. The east side of the street is occupied by several buildings that comprise the headquarters of the former Cleveland Trust Company.

This 1965 view looks north along East Ninth Street. At the upper left corner is the Cleveland Press building. The tall dark building in the distant right is the new 100 Erieview building, the first of the Erieview urban renewal projects to be completed. In the foreground is the Ohio Bell (now AT&T) Building.

The Erieview Tower was built at East 12th Street, with a plaza, fountains, trees, and a pool serving as its East Ninth entryway. The plaza was intended as a people place; the pool was converted to an ice skating rink in winter. The winds, however, that howled up East Ninth did not make the plaza very people friendly. In 1984 the plaza was replaced by the Galleria shopping mall.

This November 1965 view looks over Erieview from the east. Superior Avenue is to the left and St. Clair Avenue is to the right. At East Ninth Street, the Cuyahoga Savings (now IMG) Building is under construction. At the left Payne Avenue can still be seen running east from Superior. Payne and Walnut streets will be relocated and the block entirely rebuilt. The Diamond Building and Reserve Square Apartments will rise there.

The Markets

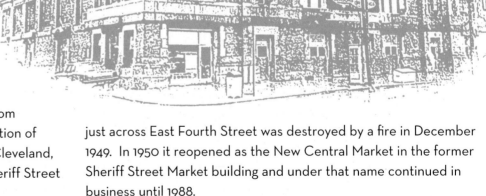

Cleveland's rapid growth during the 19th and early 20th centuries was fueled by immigration, and the city became known for its ethnic diversity.

A key component of that diversity was the preference for foods "like what we had back home."

Street-corner grocery stores carried the dietary staples but did not have the shelf or cooler space to stock a large variety of ethnic favorites. To secure these, Clevelanders made a trip to the market.

Today for most Clevelanders, "market" is synonymous with the West Side Market at West 25th Street and Lorain Avenue. It has survived competition from the supermarket chains and continues today as a destination of choice for gourmet cooks and ethnic food aficionados. Cleveland, however, once had other markets, and the downtown Sheriff Street Market and the Central Market did a thriving business.

The Sheriff Street Market operated from 1891 until 1936. It gained a second lease on life when the Central Market building just across East Fourth Street was destroyed by a fire in December 1949. In 1950 it reopened as the New Central Market in the former Sheriff Street Market building and under that name continued in business until 1988.

The city's largest chain of grocery stores during the first half of the 20th Century was
Fisher Brothers (later Fisher Foods). By 1940 Fisher had opened larger "supermarkets,"
but Cleveland's older market places continued strong.

Just about every available shelf and counter space in a typical Fisher Brothers grocery store was crammed with staples. Space limitations in these types of stores, however, made it unlikely that they could provide the variety of merchandise that some shoppers were seeking.

The West Side market has been in existence since 1840. In 1912 the City of Cleveland built this building for the market, whose significance is recognized by its inclusion as a National Historic Landmark. *(Cleveland Press Collection)*

Today's East Fourth Street was called Sheriff Street until 1906, and so the market house built on its eastern side (the building with the cupola towers at each end) was named the Sheriff Street Market. Built in 1891, the market continued in business until 1936. The site was later bought by the Gateway Economic Development Corporation, and the land was cleared and became part of the plot for the new Gateway arena and baseball facilities.

As this view shows, the Central Market was nestled in an island made by the intersection of Woodland and Broadway avenues, East Fourth and Ontario streets. This building for the market dated from 1867.

Several east side streetcar lines ran adjacent to the Central Market, a convenience factor that greatly contributed to the market's success.

It was customary for markets to offer interested vendors outdoor booths, which were particularly popular for produce merchants. Central Market had these stands along both the Ontario and East Fourth sides.

Amusement Parks

For the past half century there has been a trend in the amusement park industry that has resulted in larger but fewer parks. Many smaller amusement parks dating to the early years of the 20th Century have faded into history. Cleveland once had three such parks.

Luna Park was located between Quincy and Woodland avenues at Woodhill Road. It was served by three different streetcar lines, an important factor in park success in a time when most people traveled by public transit. The park opened in 1905, and its flashy architecture and intricate lighting gave it a magical appeal. Besides its rides, the park also had a large dance hall, games of chance, staged shows, and beer.

To certain segments of the city, some of the shows seemed a bit risqué while others objected to the park's sale of beer. For others, though, these were the appealing features. Luna Park's first two decades were quite successful, but then the onset of the Prohibition era cut the park's revenues. Debts began to mount. Luna Park closed at the end of the 1928 season.

Puritas Springs Park, Cleveland's west side amusement park, was established in 1898 and situated on Puritas Avenue at the Rocky River Reservation. Its vital transportation link was via the Cleveland and Southwestern interurban railroad. The park was purchased in 1901 by John Gooding, and it was under his leadership that the small picnic ground developed into a complete amusement park.

In addition to the rides, the park had a large dance hall and a roller skating rink. Perhaps the park is best remembered for its Cyclone roller coaster, built in 1928, and billed as the longest coaster in the country.

Patronage began to dwindle in the 1950s, and the park closed in 1958.

Euclid Beach Park was situated on the Lake Erie shore, at East 156th Street and Lake Shore Boulevard. Founded in 1895, the park's heyday began when it was purchased by the Humphrey family in 1901. The Humphrey code was "nothing to degrade or demoralize." The park prohibited alcoholic beverages and enforced a code that maintained decorum among its patrons. It was a family park.

Besides selling their famous popcorn and taffy treats, the Humphreys were determined to build a total amusement park. The Beach had a theater, dance hall, skating rink, bathhouse, and a fishing pier. It also had a kiddieland and the standard thrill rides, but it was probably most famous for its four roller coasters.

The park's last profitable year was 1963, and it closed forever after the 1969 season.

This ornate entrance arch greeted patrons to Luna Park. It bears the legend "Ingersoll's." The park was owned and built by the Ingersoll Amusement Company and remained one of its properties until 1911 when it was sold to local interests.

This aerial view shows Luna Park's "Shoot the Chutes" ride and the lagoon at the bottom of its ramp. The ride was a signature Ingersoll attraction and was duplicated in several of his parks around the country.

Puritas Springs' Cyclone roller coaster could be daunting. It took advantage of the park's location on the edge of the Rocky River ravine, and the plunge into it gave most riders more thrills than they were expecting. *(Cleveland Press Collection)*

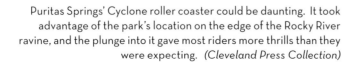

Puritas Springs is quiet in this winter scene. Cleveland amusement parks typically were open from May through September. The seven months of down time gave park personnel a chance to do needed maintenance. *(Cleveland Press Collection)*

A fire struck Puritas Spring in spring 1959, damaging The Bug and several other rides and attractions. Closed the previous year, the park became the target of trespassers and vandals. The remainder of the park was razed in 1960.

A stone archway formed the automobile entrance to Euclid Beach Park. Here the parking lot looks full, but more cars are still entering. There was auxiliary parking to the right.

In the early years of the park, patrons could take the ferry from downtown Cleveland to the Euclid Beach pier. They could also take public transit to the park which had a separate entrance for streetcars and a double-track loop.

This aerial view of the Euclid Beach layout shows where most of the rides were located. In the right foreground are the Aero Dips roller coaster and the Dance Hall. The circular building with the open center housed the Racing Derby. The Flying Turns, Thriller, and Racing Coaster are clustered center left. Across Lake Shore Boulevard is Humphrey Field, site of the park's softball diamonds.

The Thriller (left) and the Racing Coaster were built during the 1920s and remained popular attractions for the remainder of the park's years.

Over the Falls was the park's water ride. After a trip through a tunnel with occasional fantasy scenes, a boat would be hauled up to the top of the hill where it would then plunge down to the water trough below, giving riders a good splash. The Over the Falls hill, while not the highest, was Euclid Beach's steepest.

The dizzying Bubble Bounce ride was located between the Over the Falls
and the Surprise House.   It was replaced in 1957 with the Rotor.

At the eastern end of the park midway were the toboggan-like Flying Turns and the Rock-o-Plane rides.
Beyond them were the Euclid Beach Campgrounds, which had several streets of rental cottages.

Each spring season Euclid Beach Park officials would put up an eagerly awaited "Open for the Season" sign. At summer's end would appear a "Closed for the Season" sign. After September 28, 1969, the "closed" sign told the whole story.

After the park's final year, some rides were dismantled and put into storage for eventual use in the Humphrey's short-lived Shady Lake Park in Aurora. Other parts of the park succumbed to vandals who set the old dance hall aflame in 1972. The remainder of the park was then demolished, and its western portion became an apartment and nursing complex.